SOCIAL ANXIETY:

Stories Of Those With Social Anxiety
And How They Overcame Shyness

By

Grant Anderson

Copyright © 2015 Grant Anderson

All rights reserved. No part of this publication may be reproduced or transmitted in any form or by any means, electronic or mechanical, including photocopying, recording, or by any information storage and retrieval system, without permission in writing from the publisher.

Table of Contents

Introduction 4

CHAPTER ONE: 6

An Introduction To Social Anxiety 6

   An Introduction to Social Anxiety 7

   How Does Social Anxiety Get Diagnosed 9

   My Life With Social Anxiety 10

CHAPTER TWO 12

Social Anxiety Treatments & Medications 12

   A Guide to Social Anxiety Treatments 13

   A Guide to Social Anxiety Medications 26

CHAPTER THREE 29

Social Anxiety Setbacks & Maintaining Your Progress 29

   Social Anxiety Setbacks 30

   Maintaining Your Progress 33

CHAPTER FOUR 34

Social Anxiety Triggers And Stories on How People Were Able to Overcome Them 34

   Social Anxiety Triggers And Stories on How People Were Able to Overcome Them 35

Conclusion 43

BONUS #1 – FREE EBOOK 44

BONUS #2 – $20 OFF VOUCHER FOR GOALSETTINGCHALLENGE.COM 45

Introduction

First off, I'd like to thank you for purchasing "Social Anxiety: Stories of Those With Social Anxiety And How They Overcame Shyness". By getting this book you or someone you love is most likely suffering from some form of social anxiety. You've taken a good first step. Social anxiety is a terrible burden to millions of people worldwide but it can be overcome with hard work and determination.

I've personally suffered from social anxiety for most of my adult life. I have a hard time going out and having social interactions without a wave of anxiety washing over me. Just the thought of doing something is often enough to trigger an attack. Over the years I've found some effective ways to deal with my social anxiety disorder. I'm here to tell you that if I can do it, so can you. It won't be easy and your anxiety may never completely subside. However, putting the methods discussed in this book into use will help to ease your symptoms, and allow you to go out into the world living life as it's meant to be lived.

So what is social anxiety? Well, social anxiety is a disorder that can have a debilitating effect on the person suffering from it. Oftentimes the suffer is thrown into a state of extreme and unreasonable fear at the thought of being in what most people would consider normal social situations. Things like drinking or eating in front of others, or going to parties may feel impossible to a person with social anxiety.

People who suffer from social anxiety often think that they'll be humiliated or look bad when in front of other people. They begin to feel the negative effects of anxiety just thinking about being in social situations. Just the thought of going out can cause an attack. Victims of this disorder are often plagued with distorted thinking and negative outlooks on how being

Introduction

out in public will play out.

This book will share with you some stories of people like me who've lived with social anxiety and have learned to manage it. I'll go over the methods they used to overcome their issues. I hope their experiences and how they managed to push through the fear will inspire you to do the same.

Let's get started!

CHAPTER ONE:

An Introduction To Social Anxiety

In this chapter, you will learn:

- An Introduction to Social Anxiety
- How Does Social Anxiety Get Diagnosed
- My Life With Social Anxiety

An Introduction to Social Anxiety

Throughout the course of this book I will present stories of people who suffer from social anxiety and I'll share with you how they were able to persevere through adversity and come out the other side a happier and better functioning person. These stories will break down each of the main triggers into separate sections and show what methods they used to overcome each of those triggers.

First, however, I'd like to share a little more about social anxiety and what the main triggers are, along with some of the symptoms they can cause in those affected.

Social anxiety is the third most prevalent mental disorder after alcohol and depression. It affects around 20 million people a year. It usually first begins to surface in a person's teenage years or during early adulthood.

No single reason for social anxiety has ever been proven but most experts believe it's brought on by a combination of factors. These include biological factors, like how your brain pathways are wired, psychological factors like experiencing a humiliating or embarrassing trauma, and environmental factors, such as being overprotected as a youth and not forming the proper skills to deal with social situations.

Some of the main triggers include:

Being teased and made fun of by people

Drinking or eating around people

Going to work

Public speaking

Using public restrooms

Taking tests or exams

Social Anxiety

Conversations on the phone

Being at the center of attention

Hanging out with peers or going on dates

Meeting a new person

Participating in group activities

Thinking about having to go out in public

As you can see just from the short list of triggers above, this is a disorder that can ruin the lives of those suffering from it. Being paralyzed with fear is no way to live a life. It took me a long time to get comfortable doing the things listed above. At first it was a struggle to overcome my shyness and anxiety but the more things I did on this list, the easier it got.

Some of the main emotional symptoms include:

Extreme fear when being judged or watched by others

Fear that other people will see how nervous you are

Fear that you're embarrassing or humiliating yourself

Excessively self conscious and anxious in routine social situations

Worrying far in advance for upcoming events or social situations

Some of the main physical symptoms include:

Pounding heart

Shaking & sweating

Confusion

Nausea and diarrhea

Chapter One: An Introduction To Social Anxiety

Red face and blushing

Feeling short of breath

Feeling dizzy and faint

Some of the main behavioral symptoms include:

Avoiding social interactions to the point that it negatively affects your life

Hiding in the background or staying quiet in order to keep from being noticed or embarrassed

Drinking before any social situation in order to calm your shaky nerves

I've experienced most of these symptoms at some point during my struggle with anxiety. Some of them are easier to overcome than others. At times I still experience some of these symptoms. However, now I have the tools to deal with my disorder and I find that attacks are much less frequent and milder when they do occur.

How Does Social Anxiety Get Diagnosed

So you're not sure if you or a loved one has social anxiety but you know there's a problem. Maybe you have a few of the symptoms above and want to know if this disorder might be the cause of your issues.

First you'll want to visit your doctor. They'll give you a physical evaluation and ask you questions regarding your medical history. Once a physical related illness is ruled out, you'll get referred to a psychologist or psychiatrist who has special training for diagnosing and caring for these type of mental disorders.

While there is no simple test to diagnose someone with a social anxiety disorder, the doctor will use a review process and special assessment tools in order to help determine a diagnosis. The doctor will then determine if the amount of dysfunction and the severity of symptoms indicate that you're suffering from a social anxiety disorder.

My Life With Social Anxiety

I always felt anxious when I was growing up. My parents said I would throw tantrums anytime we were going somewhere with a lot of people around. While I don't recall this myself, I do remember around 7th grade really noticing my issues intensify and worsen.

It was around this time when I no longer wanted to go to school or play with friends. I even tried to quit my Saturday morning bowling team, and I was obsessed with bowling when I was younger. All I wanted to do was stay at home and play video games.

While I'm sure a lot of 7th graders felt this way, it was the degree that I didn't want to do these things that alarmed my parents. I would actually get physically upset most mornings getting ready for the bus. The symptoms often manifested in different ways. The thought of getting on the bus and facing all my classmates was utterly terrifying. It's a hard feeling to explain, but being in a constant state of distress was really having a negative affect on my well being.

For the next 5 years I would continue this cycle of anxiety attacks and acting out. My parents were old school and didn't really believe in or understand psychiatry so I was mostly left to my own devices. I tried to cope as best I could but this was not a happy period in my life.

Chapter One: An Introduction To Social Anxiety

It wasn't until my freshman year of college and learning about abnormal psychology, that I began to realize maybe there's something else going on I need to have checked out. This was many years ago, before social anxiety disorder was well known. Prior to college, I had always just internalized my feelings as best as possible and tried to tough things out. Once I saw that maybe I had other options, I got checked out. Eventually, I was diagnosed with a social anxiety disorder and began treatment.

I want to stress that I didn't start to get better immediately as it took some time for me to figure out what coping methods worked for me. I never went the medicinal route just because there weren't many options back when I was first diagnosed. During the course of this book I'll touch on various different methods to help you fight back. I urge you to try each and see which ones make the most positive impact in your life.

While my case isn't as extreme as many of the other people I've met over the years since learning about my diagnosis, it did hold me back from doing a lot of things normal kids my age were doing. Growing up I had few friends, the thought of dating sounded petrifying, and going out in public for social situations was only done out of necessity.

Now as an adult I lead a full social life, I have a great relationship with my wife, and I've learned to enjoy most (not all) social situations. I still have anxiety at times, and once in awhile that old feeling of dread grabs a hold of me and doesn't want to let go. However, I've learned ways to overcome my anxiety and that means it's possible that you can to.

CHAPTER TWO

Social Anxiety Treatments & Medications

In this chapter, you will learn:

- A Guide to Social Anxiety Treatments

- A Guide to Social Anxiety Medications

A Guide to Social Anxiety Treatments

In this section I'm going to touch on the different forms of social anxiety treatments available. For each section I'm going to go over a form of treatment and then share a story of someone I've known and relate how they've used those treatments to improve their lives.

1. Challenging Negative Thoughts

People who suffer from a social phobia have negative beliefs and thoughts that help fuel their anxiety. Many have thoughts that others find them stupid, or that if they try something they'll fail and embarrass themselves. In this treatment, you're taught to question these negative thoughts and challenge their validity.

You can either try this on your own or in therapy. I highly recommend anyone just diagnosed to start with therapy. A therapist will have a wealth of knowledge to share with you and can give you the guidance needed to be successful.

If you want to do it on your own I would use the following information to guide you. The first step you need to take is to identify your negative thoughts that automatically come up any time a social situation occurs. For example, if you have a speech to give, an underlying negative reaction might be that you're going to embarrass yourself and everyone will think you're an idiot.

Once you've determined the negative thoughts you need to begin analyzing and challenging them. Begin by asking yourself some questions about your negative thoughts: "Do I really know that I'm going to embarrass myself?" "Will people really think I'm an idiot over a bad speech?" By evaluating your negative thoughts you're able to begin replacing them with more positive and realistic ways of viewing the social situa-

Social Anxiety

tions triggering your anxiety.

Another thing you'll want to start doing is determining if you're engaging in distorted thinking or unhelpful styles of thinking. Ther are a few main categories of these types of thinking which I'll briefly go over.

Fortune telling – Always predicting bad outcomes for upcoming situations. You get so worked up at the possibility of things not working out you're anxious before the situation even occurs.

Mind reading – You start to think you know how other people feel about you and it's normally in the same negative way you view yourself.

Personalizing – Thinking that everyone is negatively focusing on you and that any problems other people have going on in their lives is directly tied to you.

Catastrophic thinking – Always blowing up things bigger than they are. You make molehills into mountains. Small issues feel like the end of the world.

So how can you begin to stop these forms of thinking from overwhelming you? Well, the more time you spend focusing outward and paying attention to your surroundings, the less time you'll spend inwardly focusing on your anxiety symptoms.

Try really listening to what other people are saying and not all the negative thoughts you normally focus on. Remember to try and be present in conversations and really look at and engage with the people you're surrounded by. If there's a pause in a conversation don't feel pressured to keep it going. A little silence is fine; people won't think less of you.

When in social situations the more time you spend interact-

Chapter Two: Social Anxiety Treatments & Medications

ing, the less time you'll have to internalize your anxiety. While this may not cause your anxiety to vanish, it can lessen the symptoms and hold it has over you. Also, remember to challenge any negative thoughts as they happen. Once you begin to do this regularly it will become a habit that will help you immeasurably throughout life.

Debra's Story

Debra was a "worry wart since birth" as her mother would like to say. All through her teen years she constantly worried over every little detail of her life. Her mom was always there to calm her down, so while it was hard, she was able to manage.

However, soon after finishing up her schooling at a local college, she got offered a great job in the medical profession. The one catch was it was in a neighboring state. She accepted the position and moved to a new small town.

Once there she began to find herself worrying about every detail of her life. From if the clothes she wore made her look weird, to if she was even qualified to have the great job she got offered.

How was she going to handle all her new responsibilities and meet new people? Eventually the spiral of negative thinking turned into a full-blown anxiety attack. It was at this point Debra realized she needed some help even her mother couldn't provide.

Debra quickly found a local psychologist and was soon after diagnosed with a social anxiety disorder. With some therapy, Debra learned her main issue was allowing her negative thoughts to go unchecked and overwhelm her until she could think of nothing else. Debra's psychologist started having her write down and record her thoughts and challenge them as they were occurring. She had to step back and take a moment to examine each thought in a rational manner and decide whether this was an actual concern or her anxiety talking.

It wasn't long before Debra had learned to control her "stinkin thinkin". Not her term but what her psychologist liked to refer to all negative thoughts as. Over time Debra was able to stop her anxious feelings and worrying before they were able to gain any real momentum. She was able to apply the tools she learned and improve every facet of her life. She made new friends, started a meaningful relationship, even went on vacations to tourist destinations filled with strangers. Debra learned that she can't control every situation, but she can control her thoughts, actions and attitude. Now the only thing that gets her anxious is the thought of fitting into her wedding dress one day.

2. Learning to Control Your Breath

There are a lot of changes that occur in your body once you get anxious. The first thing to normally happen is you begin to start breathing quickly. Breathing too quickly will throw off your carbon dioxide and oxygen balance leading to more anxiety symptoms starting. These symptoms include things such as increased heart rate, dizziness, feeling like you might suffocate, and painful muscle tension.

By learning to properly control your breath when worked up from negative thinking, you can get the physical symptoms related to your anxiety under control. Practice this breathing exercise to help you stay calm when you're in social situations or are the center of attention.

Sit comfortably; straighten up your back while keeping your shoulders both relaxed. Then place a hand on your stomach and the other on your chest.

Chapter Two: Social Anxiety Treatments & Medications

Inhale deeply and slowly through only your nose. Do this for about four seconds. The hand you have on your stomach should be rising, while the other hand should only move minimally.

Hold your breath for about 2 seconds. Then exhale through your mouth slowly for about 6 more seconds. You want to push as much air out as possible. The hand placed on your stomach will be moving in while your exhaling and the other hand should only be moving a minimal amount

Continue repeating this process and keep your focus on maintaining a steady pattern of breathing. To simplify it's 4 in followed by hold for 2 and then 6 out.

In addition to this breathing technique I've shown you, it would be a good idea to regularly practice a few different relaxation techniques. I would try yoga and meditation and see how much benefit you find in them. I personally don't like yoga but I quite enjoy the time I set aside each day to mediate. Do whatever works best for you.

Madison's Story

Madison grew up with a wonderful family who supported her dreams and spared no expense to make her happy. However, she always seemed to have a rougher time with things than most other kids she knew. Madison was like most girls, she loved singing and going shopping for clothes, but something always felt a little off and different. From an early age her aunts would joke that they half expected her to get an ulcer before high school with the amount of anxiety and worry she had. Madison spent many school days lying down in the nurse's office with a stomach issue. It wasn't till many years later she learned why.

Her first serious anxiety attack happened during college. She

Social Anxiety

was at the movies with friends and suddenly she couldn't breathe and she felt dizzy and nauseous. Madison ended up in urgent care that night, getting every test imaginable. The doctors found nothing physically wrong and she thought she had gone crazy. This happened two more times before a doctor finally clued her into anxiety disorders. It was at this point Madison sought out help provided by her school to students in need.

Madison began regularly seeing a psychologist who gave her some advice that changed her life. She told her to run. The psychologist explained that running is a great way to learn breath control. Madison took her advice and transformed her life.

Now graduated from college and out on her own in the world. Madison has her anxiety under control. With the help of running, yoga, and counseling she has learned how to stop her anxiety before it can ever rear its ugly head.

3. Facing Your Fears

A great method for treating your social anxiety disorder and overcoming your issues is to face the things you fear instead of actively avoiding them. Avoidance only helps to fuel your disorder.

Avoiding your problems will only lead to even more problems. I know avoidance can lead to some short-term relief, especially when gripped with fear and anxiety. However, by constantly avoiding social situations you're preventing yourself from ever getting comfortable in them. In fact, it has been shown that more avoidance to scary social situations leads to it becoming even more frightening over time.

Avoidance will also keep you from enjoying your life to it's fullest and attaining your goals. For example, having a speak-

Chapter Two: Social Anxiety Treatments & Medications

ing phobia can prevent you from meeting new friends, and being more successful in the workplace. By facing that fear head on, you can learn to overcome it, but if you always avoid public speaking your situation will never have a chance at improving.

While overcoming your fears may feel impossible, try doing things in small steps. The key is to begin with a scenario that you can deal with, and slowly work your way towards more difficult situations. By slowly building up your coping skills and confidence you'll be able to move higher up the anxiety ladder.

For example, if you get nervous talking to strangers, you may want to try going to a party with a friend. Once you're comfortable with that, you may want to try engaging one stranger in a conversation.

Continue to set new goals for overcoming your anxiety and gradually check each one off the list. I suggest GoalSetting-Challenge.com if you need an easy-to-follow spreadsheet that pushes you to complete your goals (see BONUS #2). Start small and work up to the things you're frightened of the most. If you try and bite off too much too fast, you'll likely fail and only help to reinforce the anxiety.

Overcoming fear takes time. Patience is a virtue. Use all the previous skills you've learned above like challenging negative thoughts and controlling your breathing to increase your odds of long term success.

Ryan's Story

Ryan's story starts off the same way as many other people suffering with social anxiety. He had his first anxiety attack at 14. A few years later he would get them whenever driving on the freeway. He would get them in public places like the mall

Social Anxiety

and grocery store. By the time he had reached his early twenties he stopped going to most places altogether. Within a few more years he never went anywhere by himself.

Ryan quit his job and found a way to work from home. He sold his car and had to rely on his wife to accompany him whenever they did have to leave the house. Finally Ryan got the courage to get some help and after some time with a therapist decided to start confronting his fears head on.

Ryan made a list of things he was afraid to do and put them in order from least to most frightening. The first step was being alone at the movies. Once he had mastered that it was being alone at the grocery store. This went on for a few months before he finally managed to courage to face his fear of driving. Ryan wasn't always successful on his first try but he didn't let anything set him back for long. If he failed he simply tried again another day.

Ryan still suffers from anxiety attacks at times and progress can feel slow, but if you look at his list you'll see he's light years ahead of where he started off. His comfort zone is much larger and he's able to function and feel comfortable in most social situations. Ryan took his life back by facing his fears. I urge you to do the same.

4. Build Stronger Relationships

Another excellent treatment for social anxiety is actively going out and becoming a member of supportive situations. Here are some helpful ways of interacting with other people in a positive manner.

Try volunteering. It should be something you think you'll enjoy. Some examples are working at a shelter, stuffing envelopes for someone's political campaign, anything that gives you some type of activity to stay focused on, yet still engaging

Chapter Two: Social Anxiety Treatments & Medications

with at least a few like-minded individuals.

You can also take a class. Something that focuses on assertiveness training or social skills might of value. You can find these types of classes being offered at most community colleges and adult education centers.

Actively try and work on communicating better. Strong healthy relationships are dependent on clear and intelligent communication. When you have trouble connecting with other people, learning some new emotional intelligence skills would be beneficial.

Ava's Story

Ava has struggled with her social anxiety disorder for the last 30 years. It started as teenager. At first her parents thought her extreme mood swings and loner attitude were just a phase she was going through. However, eventually her conditions worsened and they decided to bring her to a psychiatrist. Unfortunately the psychiatrist said her problems were a result of poor treatment from her family, which in Ava's mind was the furthest thing from the truth. This incident steered her away from seeking treatment for another 10 years. Her life continued to spiral downward.

At 25, Ava had a complete breakdown. Her self-esteem was non existent, her head was full of false beliefs, and she had turned to alcohol as a form of avoidance. She couldn't bring herself to go out of her house even when it was for something important. Ava had reached her breaking point.

While being treated at the hospital, a doctor diagnosed her with social anxiety disorder and alcoholism. She was referred to a counselor who gave her the tools to change her outlook on life and begin to heal. Ava's doctor suggested she join AA not only for her drinking but because being part of a social

Social Anxiety

group would allow her to face her fears and overcome her negative thinking.

Slowly things began to take a turn for the better. Ava enjoyed the support group setting so she joined a few other similar groups and found it helped her socialize and begin to feel comfortable in her skin. She took classes on anxiety, public speaking and how to develop interpersonal skills. From there she branched out into classes on things she enjoyed like cooking and crafting.

After five years of hard work Ava had replaced her unhealthy set of beliefs with rational healthy beliefs, and had learned to trust others. Ava replaced unhealthy coping mechanisms, like drinking and replaced them with engaging healthy social activities and support groups. Now she runs a social anxiety support group and for the first time in her life has developed a feeling of self worth for the woman she's become.

5. Change Your Lifestyle

While simply changing your lifestyle isn't enough on its own to overcome a social phobia, it can work as a great supporting treatment used in conjunction with some or all of the treatments discussed above. The following treatment tips will enable you to lower your anxiety level and lead a more centered life.

Limit or avoid caffeine. Things like tea, coffee, caffeinated soda, chocolate and energy drinks all are stimulants that can increase the symptoms of anxiety.

Limit your consumption of alcohol. You may want to have a few drinks when out in a social situation as a means of avoidance but alcohol actually increases the risk of anxiety attacks.

Stop smoking. Nicotine happens to be a strong stimulant.

Chapter Two: Social Anxiety Treatments & Medications

Smoking actually raises not lowers your anxiety level.

Get a proper amount of sleep. If you're deprived of sleep, you're at a higher risk of having an anxiety attack. Staying well rested can help you stay relaxed when out in social situations.

Tony's Story

Tony didn't start suffering from social anxiety until later in life. He had his first attack shortly after the birth of his first child. Tony began to notice his anxiety got worse whenever he was alone with his newborn son. He became terrified something bad was going to happen if they left the house. Soon, Tony started getting anxious in other social situations. He had multiple attacks at work and one anxiety attack got so bad he went to the hospital convinced he was having a heart attack.

Luckily for Tony, the doctors treating him found nothing physically wrong and recognized the symptoms he was explaining. Tony soon saw the psychiatrist referred to him and learned that he was suffering from a social anxiety disorder. When describing his symptoms and explaining when his attacks normally occurred, Tony's doctor realized that his lifestyle had recently changed with the birth of his son. No longer was Tony getting a full night sleep like he used to, but he had stopped exercising altogether, and on top of that he had been guzzling energy drinks at work loaded with caffeine to stay awake.

Tony's doctor advised him that these negative lifestyle changes may have been exacerbating his anxiety attacks. Tony quickly cut out caffeine, found time to exercise again, and made a point to get more sleep each evening. Within a month, Tony's anxiety was greatly reduced and he wasn't having any more full on anxiety attacks. He still needs work on control-

Social Anxiety

ling his negative thinking, and he struggles with being out in public with his son alone, but by making some small adjustments to his everyday routine, Tony was able to dramatically improve the quality of his life.

6. CBT - Cognitive Behavioral Therapy

If none of the self help treatments above are enough to help you gain some control over your social anxiety disorder, the best professional treatment is (CBT) or cognitive behavioral therapy.

This type of therapy believes in the premise that the things you think about affect the way you feel, and those feelings end up affecting your behavior. This means if you're able to successfully change your thinking about the social situations that cause anxiety, you'll end up feeling and functioning better.

> CBT involves learning ways to control your physical anxiety symptoms using breathing exercises and relaxation techniques.

> CBT involves challenging your unhelpful, negative thoughts that trigger and help to fuel your social anxiety, and replaces them with rational and balanced views.

> CBT involves confronting your fear of social situations in a systemic, gradual way, instead of avoiding them.

> CBT involves following the advice and guidance of your therapist and applying the lessons they teach you into your daily routine. CBT can also involve group therapy sessions where you role-play and hone your social skills along with other members of the group.

Chapter Two: Social Anxiety Treatments & Medications

While in group therapy, they may use things like mock interviews, recording you on tape, acting drills, and observing other group members, all as different exercises to simulate what makes you get anxious when out among people in the real world. The more you prepare and practice for these real life situations that cause you anxiety, the more confident and comfortable you'll grow over time, which in turn will lead to less anxiety.

Roger's Story

Roger had been diagnosed with social anxiety at an early age. Over the years he had tried the self-help treatments above to limited success. Things would seem to be turning around for him and then out of the blue his anxiety would spike and he would spiral out of control for longer and longer periods of time.

Roger had seen a therapist as a kid but didn't have good memories about the experience so he resisted getting professional help for many years. His long time and long suffering girlfriend eventually put her foot down and all but dragged him to a therapist practicing CBT.

His girlfriend was a member of a social anxiety forum and saw how many people benefited from this type of treatment, so off Roger went begrudgingly and as skeptical as ever. At first, Roger had a hard time seeing the value of therapy. Many of the techniques being suggested he had tried and failed with on his own over the years. Roger soon realized, however, that he needed to put his best foot forward for the sake of his girlfriend and a chance at some inner tranquility.

Roger's therapist suggested group therapy and that's where things began to click. At first Roger was terrified of the idea of opening up and sharing with other strangers. What would they think of him? After a few sessions he began to get com-

Social Anxiety

fortable and the process began to take hold.

It's been 8 years since Roger first started therapy. Now he goes to maintain his own anxiety levels and help others just starting out who are unsure of the process like he was all those years ago. Roger still has issues in many social situations. You'll never catch him in a public restroom for one thing. However, the list of anxiety triggers dwindles down a little each passing year and Roger has found a way to live with his disorder and not get overcome by it.

A Guide to Social Anxiety Medications

Sometimes treatment alone isn't enough to control a social anxiety disorder. Medication is used at times to help relieve symptoms of social anxiety. The problem with this is that medication is only temporary. There is no cure for this disorder so once you stop taking your medication your anxiety symptoms will normally return at full force.

Using medication is often considered to be most helpful if used in addition to some form of therapy or self help treatment. Medication is good for taking the edge off, but dealing with the root cause of your disorder is the best method for lessening your anxiety in the long run.

There are 3 main types of medication that are used for treating social anxiety disorders:

Antidepressants – These are good for extreme cases of social anxiety where the anxiety is debilitating and severe. There are currently three different antidepressants currently approved for treating social phobias by the Food and Drug Administration. These are Effexor, Zoloft and Paxil.

Beta-blockers – This medication is used for relieving the symptoms of performance anxiety. Beta-blockers work by blocking our flow of adrenaline, which occurs whenever we're anxious. While beta-blockers won't help the emotional anxiety symptoms, they will help control physical anxiety symptoms like sweating, shaky voice and hands, dizziness and rapid heartbeat.

Benzodiazepines – These are a fast acting and powerful anti anxiety medication. These are normally only prescribed if the above medications haven't worked due to them being an addictive sedative. If you're not careful with this medication, it can do more harm then good.

Tisha's Story

Tisha was at the end of her rope. She had been suffering from a severe case of social anxiety since her early teens. She had dropped out of high school due to her constant anxiety attacks and wasn't able to get a job until the Internet started offering opportunities to work from home.

The only friends Tisha had left were mainly online, as most of her friends eventually got tired of always having to come to her house in order to see her. They had grown up, moved away and had families of their own. Tisha had been in therapy on and off since high school but even the visit to the therapist was overwhelming most of the time. Tisha had even tried medication for a short time but it didn't seem to have much affect. Nothing seemed to do the job.

Eventually someone in one the forums she was a member of suggested she try the medication again but this time do it in conjunction with CBT. In the past, she had done both, but never both at the same time. Tisha decided enough was enough and took the forum member's advice.

It took some time to get the medications right and a treatment schedule she was comfortable with but Tisha has begun to make a lot of forward progress. She's able to interact in

Social Anxiety

more and more social settings, although she still doesn't drive or have a job outside of her home yet. Those are both on her list however, and in time she's confident she'll be able to cross everything off the list. Even possibly move out on her own one day.

Tisha knows that the medication while helpful is only a stop-gap solution. She's made a concerted effort to face her fears one by one and conquer them. It might take a few more years before she has her anxiety fully under control but she believes she can accomplish it. That kind of positive mindset speaks volumes and means she's finally winning the battle.

CHAPTER THREE

Social Anxiety Setbacks & Maintaining Your Progress

In this chapter, you will learn:

- Social Anxiety Setbacks

- Maintaining Your Progress

Social Anxiety Setbacks

Slip ups or setbacks in your progress can happen at a moments notice and are honestly to be expected. Don't let yourself fall into the belief that you're starting back at square one. This type of thinking will only make you feel even worse and increase your anxiety levels. Change is not always a straight line. Sometimes you'll take a step back before moving two more steps forward.

For example, think of how you learned to ride a bike when you were little. It probably took a few attempts and a couple of spills before you learned to balance and stay upright. Even then, when you rode over different surfaces sometimes you became unsteady and had to regain your balance. Developing a new skill set isn't an easy process. There will always be new challenges that arise, and you'll need to learn how to adapt your skills to overcome them.

There are several common reasons for setbacks occurring. When you have an increase in mental or physical stress, you're more prone to slip and let your anxiety get the best of you. When you're feeling under the weather, it can be difficult to maintain your composure and fight off and dispute your negative and unhelpful thoughts.

Try and always remind yourself that it's alright to have a "down day" and that all people have them from time to time. You're only human! Try and cut yourself a little slack. Try using the skills you've learned to challenge those negative thoughts when they occur. You should also use your setbacks as a lesson to learn more about yourself, and think of how you can avoid a similar situation from occurring in the future.

As you start to get deep into your treatment and are beginning to progress through the goals you've set, realize the setbacks you face are just a blip on the radar. Something that

CHAPTER THREE: Social Anxiety Setbacks & Maintaining Your

won't matter in a day, week or month from now.

If you start to notice that you're facing smaller setbacks on a more frequent basis, here are some things you may want to do in order to prevent a major setback from happening.

Identify the early warning symptoms and signs. A few common examples of these are when you start spending an increased amount of your time trying to avoid social situations. You see a noticeable increase in your physical anxiety symptoms when you're facing a social situation you previously feared. You begin having more negative and unhelpful thoughts then normal, and you're increasingly worrying about how others perceive you.

Consider revising your skills. Try and think about all the skills you've developed to reduce your anxiety (relaxation, calming and breathing techniques, challenging negative thinking). Have you been practicing these skills as often as you should? If not, you may need to increase the time spent working on them, or you may need to try and continue learning more skills.

Social support is crucial. It's very important you have someone you can sit with and have a conversation. This doesn't mean more therapy where you're pouring out your heart. It means just finding someone you can vent to and discuss your goals and what's happening in your world at that moment. Problems often seem bigger in your head. Once you begin hearing your issues out loud, it can give you some much needed perspective.

Jason's Story

Jason started having anxiety from the time he was 9 years old. He had a hard time making new friends, and while he enjoyed the outdoors, it was only as long as it was somewhere quiet

Social Anxiety

where he could be alone.

Over the years Jason saw his anxiety around groups of people continue to worsen. It went from feeling a little uncomfortable around strangers to getting panicked at the thought of going to a crowded area like a party or concert. Jason started to withdraw from everyone around him and retreated more and more into his shell.

Eventually Jason made the choice to seek assistance. He was ready for a change and grew tired of the negative thoughts ruling his life. He found that one on one therapy coupled with anti anxiety medication was what worked best for him. He began trying to work on his fear of large groups and started to make some progress. Everything seemed to be changing for the better.

Then came the first wave of setbacks. Jason was not properly prepared for this. He was just starting to feel better and then his anxiety symptoms began to get worse, and he began to let the old negative thoughts creep back in and undermine all the positive work he had been doing.

Jason began to avoid his therapy and convinced himself that it wasn't possible to feel normal. A few months passed and Jason decided to come back to therapy and his therapist really began to focus on dealing with setbacks and how to deal with things when they're not going your way. Jason took this advice to heart and really focused on using any setbacks as something he could learn from. Once he was able to view the setbacks as something he could change into a positive his progress really began to take off.

It's been about a year now and Jason is happy to report that his symptoms are much more manageable now, and although he does have at least one or two setbacks a month, he's able to look back and remember when it felt like his entire life was

Maintaining Your Progress

It's important to keep in mind all the progress you've made during your time in treatment. When you attain a goal, it's good to give yourself a little pat on the back and really try to celebrate those moments. Giving yourself positive reinforcement is a way to keep yourself encouraged to keep on practicing and applying all the new skills you've developed. Maintaining your positive gains during treatment requires you continue to confront the social situations you felt anxious in and continual to practice the skills you learned to overcome that fear.

It's a good idea to break down your life into some different areas and write out how you plan to stay well and practice your skills. For example, one area could be social activities. For this area of your life you could write that you plan to spend time with your friends at least once each week. Another area could be self-care. For this area, you could write that you plan on exercising daily and will shop for fresh fruits and vegetables every week.

As time goes on and your life changes, you'll want to continually update the areas of your life and the goals you want to attain for each one. Writing things down is a great reinforcement tool and an excellent way not to lose track of what you want to accomplish. I highly recommend you trying it. I've been doing it for a while now and I find it to be a great way to monitor my progress.

CHAPTER FOUR

Social Anxiety Triggers And Stories on How People Were Able to Overcome Them

In this chapter, you will learn:

- Social Anxiety Triggers And Stories on How People Were Able to Overcome Them

Social Anxiety Triggers And Stories on How People Were Able to Overcome Them

In this section, I plan on sharing with you some stories of how people with social anxiety disorder were able to overcome their triggers and begin to lead a healthier and happier life. I find it helpful to hear what others went through and what they did to turn their life around. If they can do it, there's no reason why anyone else can't.

Being Teased and Made Fun Of By People - Artie's Story

This is a common trigger for those suffering from anxiety. It's especially prevalent in younger kids who are the subject of more constant teasing from their peers. Artie fell into the being teased group. He was always shy and on the quiet side, so this made him an easy target for bullies and other kids at school. As he got older, Artie found himself filled with a dizzying array of intense fears and social phobias. The thought of interacting with new people, especially in groups, made him so nauseous he began to have a phobia of vomiting on them.

Over the years, Artie got treatment and had a supportive family who tried their best to understand his issues. He had a hard time finishing school but he made it through and once enrolled in college, Artie really began to take a hard look at what underlying causes were feeding his phobias and anxiety. He realized that most of his issues stemmed from his being teased and taunted growing up.

With this knowledge in hand, Artie focused on confronting this fear and with the help of group therapy and CBT was able to move past the past. Artie no longer lets the thoughts of being teased and being unlikable hold him back. Now his anxiety levels have dropped to a much more manageable level and he's able to lead a much more socially active lifestyle.

Social Anxiety

Public Speaking – Tammy's Story

Tammy is an art history researcher. Over the years she's avoided any type of scenario where she would have talk to a group of people. Her social anxiety trigger is public speaking and the thought of having to speak, to any group, was enough to cause her to get dizzy and nauseous. For years, her phobia avoidance had held her back from getting the promotions she wanted and thought she deserved. Finally, Tammy decided that if something was going to change, it would only be if she made the change happen.

Tammy began CBT and after about 6 months was comfortable enough to start trying group therapy. Once she realized she wasn't being judged and she was in a supportive environment, Tammy was really able to work on confronting her fears and developing the skills to overcome them. She would act out short plays with the group and give mock speeches. This eventually led to her working up the courage to finally speak up at work and present her research findings in a public forum. Within a year she got a small promotion and is no longer terrorized at the thought of speaking in public. She still has setbacks and the fear still lingers in the background. However, it no longer dictates what she's able to do and accomplish.

Eating Or Drinking In Public

The fear of drinking or eating in public can be a real detriment to both your professional and personal life. Most social situations include one of the two. Business meetings are often held over meals, and families usually gather over dinner to celebrate and connect with one another.

If eating or drinking while among other people causes you to have extreme anxiety, you'll either have to be very uncomfortable and endure the encounter or find a way to avoid the situation altogether. Avoidance is never the answer. It creates a cycle where the more you avoid, the harder it becomes to eat and drink in public. Over time you'll probably begin limiting not only your career choices, but also limiting your friendships and family life when suffering from this social phobia.

Some people have different eating and drinking triggers. Some get very anxious when they have to eat or drink in front of other people. Some people's fears are geared towards more specific types of events like dinner parties or formal banquets. I have a friend who can't eat in front of his parents or boss because they're an authority figure. Some can't dine in a crowded environment but are all right when dining with a couple companions in a quieter setting.

Most people with this phobia notice their anxiety rise in correlation with how difficult the food they're having is to eat. For example, a messier food like spaghetti would be more anxiety provoking then a steak, since there's a greater chance of embarrassment when eating it.

Finger foods are normally less stress inducing then foods requiring utensils. Dishes that have a sauce on them are usually among the top anxiety provoking foods. Most people don't worry about the type of beverage, just that they're going to spill it, however things like red wine may provoke more anxiety than water because of the former's ability to leave a stain.

People with this social anxiety phobia are normally afraid of a few different embarrassing things happening. These include spilling their food and drinks, choking on their food and bringing more attention to themselves, vomiting or losing control of their bowels, looking stupid or unattractive while eating, and getting flushed in the face from spicy and hot food.

Social Anxiety

Rich's Story

Rich came from a big family who liked to gather and have lots of parties and celebrations. This always made Rich intensely nervous. He didn't like anyone to pay too much attention to him. Staying in the background was where he always felt the most comfortable. Rich never thought he was as good or smart as the cousins his age were, and was convinced they were judging him on everything he did. When it came time to sit down for a meal, Rich felt the most anxiety wash over him. Now he was trapped sitting next to people who could watch and judge every bite he ate. He was always afraid he'd throw up, start choking on his food, or his hands would start shaking so bad he'd spill his drink all over himself.

Rich was too embarrassed to say anything for years, and as he got older he was able to find reasons to skip more and more of these family functions. By this point Rich tried to avoid any social setting that involved food. It wasn't until he opened up about his problem to a woman he was dating, that he got the courage to try and get help for his issues.

He went to therapist who suggested CBT and he slowly began the work of confronting his fears. First, he told his family about his condition and began by have smaller dinners and then slowly over time increasing the number of people at each get together. It took a long time but Rich is now able to find some enjoyment in family gatherings. He still has a problem going out into crowded restaurants but has recently started taking some anti anxiety medications along with continuing his therapy. Rich knows that as long as he keeps pushing forward, he'll learn to overcome his social phobia.

Working In Public – Kevin's Story

Another trigger for many people is working in a public setting. Kevin worked as a cashier at Target. The day would

Chapter Four: Social Anxiety Triggers And Stories On How People

normally start off slowly, so anxiety levels would be low. However, as the day went on and gets busier, Kevin would begin to feel pressure from the amount of customers growing in his line. The negative thoughts would begin to tell him that customers where upset with him because he wasn't working fast enough, which led to him getting nervous because if he went faster, he thought he'd start ringing items up incorrectly or give out the wrong amount of change. As a result of this anxiety, Kevin would start sweating, feeling shaky, and his heart would begin to pound. This began to make each day feel like a nightmare.

Kevin had a long history of sporadic employment. He would bounce from low-level job to low-level job, always finding a reason to quit. He tried to find jobs without too much social interaction but that wasn't always easy. Kevin also never put himself in a position to receive promotions. Even if he was more qualified than a co-worker, his fear of dealing with people in a social setting wouldn't allow him to try and achieve more. Eventually, he began to skip days at work and was fired from his cashier job. Once again unemployed, Kevin began to dread the idea of having to find another place to work.

It was around this time he realized he needed to find a way to deal with his social phobias. Going from job he hated to job he hated wasn't any way to live and he wanted to start planning for his future. He needed to find something he could do and be passionate about. He decided to seek out help and began therapy. He started learning coping mechanisms and breathing exercises he could use when he began to feel anxiety in the workplace, and he also started working in a group therapy setting to help confront his fear of social situations.

Kevin began to exercise and make some dietary changes to his lifestyle. He cut out caffeine and stopped smoking cigarettes. That, coupled with the therapy sessions and a pre-

Social Anxiety

scription to anti anxiety medication, allowed him to start dreaming bigger for himself. Kevin enrolled in a technical school and is now training to be an electrician. He hopes to one day open is own business.

Being The Center of Attention

Being at the center of attention is a very common fear for sufferers of social anxiety disorder. Although avoiding the spotlight is the comfortable thing to do when suffering from this phobia, it is only teaching you that you're incapable of handling the attention. That's simply not true! You should instead start gradually trying to introduce yourself into a situation where you know the focus will be squarely on you. Confronting your fears slowly is the best way to overcome them.

This process is often called exposure therapy. It is one of the most crucial components of CBT or cognitive behavioral treatment. A good idea is to make a list of the situations that you fear the most and rank them in order. This is often called a fear hierarchy.

Once that has been done, slowly begin tackling your list starting with the least anxiety provoking activity and work your way up to the one that scares you the most. The idea is that once you get comfortable with the first few, you'll begin to build your confidence, and you'll be better equipped to tackle the one's that frighten you the most.

When you practice these exposures, you need to fully commit. Don't try to partially avoid them by doing part of the activity and not all of it. In order for this therapy to work, you need to have fully experienced an anxiety that happens from participating in the activity.

If you don't feel you're ready to tackle a situation in real life, try to act out the situation in your head a few times. Repeat-

Chapter Four: Social Anxiety Triggers And Stories On How People

edly doing this can have a positive impact on how you'll handle these situations once out there real.

Sara's Story

Sara loved to sing and dance. However, even from an early age, the thought of doing so for an audience made her sick to her stomach. She would still continue to practice but she never felt comfortable sharing her passion with anyone else.

As she got older she had to watch her friends join drama club and marching band while she sat on the sidelines. No matter how much she wanted to be performing, her anxiety would spike, her heart would start racing and her instinct was yelling for her to flee back into the background, and avoid even thinking about what she was missing out on. Unfortunately, she listened to those negative thoughts and went through high school with out ever really taking part in the high school experience outside of class.

In college, it was more of the same during her freshman and sophomore years. She saw musical and play announcements always being put up around campus but she continued her pattern of avoidance afraid that she would look stupid and that she would never be good enough to make the cut. It wasn't until her junior year of college when one of her friends caught her singing in her room and asked why she had never tried out for anything. It was only then that Sara opened up about her social phobia issues.

Sara's friend convinced her to go see someone who could help her resolve her issues, and while it took some pressuring, she finally caved in and agreed to meet with someone on a trial basis. Sara's new therapist suggested she try CBT and also had her join group therapy for further assistance.

Sara learned to make a fear hierarchy list to help her over-

Social Anxiety

come her fears. She also got a lot of positive reinforcement letting her know that she was actually a very good singer and had a great opportunity to get cast in a school production at some point.

The idea of being on stage was her biggest trigger so she put that last on the list and began her journey with her first fear on the list, which was wearing something really flashy that would have all eyes clearly on her. She went ahead and did it but quickly failed and retreated back to the safety of her room. However, she stuck with it and tried a second time. This time she was able to accomplish her goal without letting her anxiety overcome her.

Sara spent the rest of that junior year and all of summer break knocking things off her list. By the time late fall of her senior year came around, she felt confident enough to try out for a play. She made it through the tryout successfully, and while she didn't get the role she wanted, she did get a small singing part. This was the big test. Her first performance was terrifying but she made it through, and became more comfortable with each passing performance on stage.

Now Sara is regularly involved in her community theater. While she still spends the majority of the time working on things behind the scenes, she still makes it a point to get on stage and face her fear head on, at least a few times a year. She's learned that with hard work and practice, you can learn to control your fear. She no longer allows herself to be a prisoner of her social anxiety disorder.

Conclusion

Thank you again for purchasing this book. I hope you've taken something from the stories I've shared about these courageous individuals. Each and every one of them were able to overcome their social phobia and make a life for themselves not dictated by fear.

It wasn't an easy process and it certainly didn't happen overnight. However, these people realized that if they wanted their lives to change they needed to be the ones to do the work. It may take time to find a treatment that works for you; everyone is different. You also may have setbacks from time to time. But remember to use them as a learning experience and continue pushing forward.

I hope you find the treatments and ideas presented in this book helpful. I highly recommend seeing a doctor if you think you may be suffering from a social anxiety disorder. Get diagnosed, and start a treatment tailored to your specific situation. The longer you avoid your problems, the harder they'll be to overcome down the line. No matter what age you are, now is the time to overcome it! Social anxiety is a lifetime battle but it's a battle you can win.

Good luck! I wish you all a bright and happier future!

BONUS #1 – FREE EBOOK

Go to:
http://planetearth.leadpages.co/grantanderson/

BONUS #2 – $20 OFF VOUCHER FOR GOAL-SETTINGCHALLENGE.COM

Offer code: ebook20

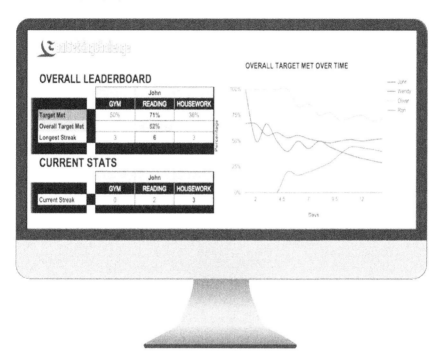

Check Out My Other Books On Amazon

DEPRESSION

STORIES OF THOSE WITH DEPRESSION AND HOW THEY HELPED THEMSELVES

G R A N T   A N D E R S O N

I Need Your Help...

I really want to thank you for reading this book. I sincerely hope that you enjoyed it and that it helped you in some way.

If you received value from this book, then I'd like to ask you for a favor. Would you be kind enough to leave a review for this book on Amazon?

I'm just starting out writing books and it's hard to get noticed being new. Getting more reviews will help me get more exposure.

I really appreciate your help :)

Thank you for your time!

Grant Anderson

Printed in Great Britain
by Amazon